ketball's MVPs

D0124781

STEVE NASH

Dan Osier

PowerKiDS press

New York

Published in 2011 by The Rosen Publishing Group, Inc.
29 East 21st Street, New York, NY 10010

Copyright © 2011 by The Rosen Publishing Group, Inc.

First Edition

Editor: Amelie von Zumbusch
Book Design: Kate Laczynski

Photo Credits: Cover, p. 1 Kevin C. Cox/Getty Images; pp. 4, 7
Noah Graham/NBAE/Getty Images; pp. 8, 16 Barry Gossage/
NBAE/Getty Images; p. 11 Mike Hewitt/Getty Images; p. 12
Fernando Medina/NBAE/Getty Images; p. 15 Otto Greule Jr./G
Images; pp. 18–19 Lisa Blumenfeld/Getty Images; p. 20 D. Clar
Evans/NBAE/Getty Images; p. 22 Sam Forencich/NBAE/Getty
Images.

Library of Congress Cataloging-in-Publication Data

Osier, Dan.
  Steve Nash / by Dan Osier.
    p. cm. — (Basketball's MVPs)
  Includes index.
  ISBN 978-1-4488-2525-7 (library binding) —
  ISBN 978-1-4488-2634-6 (pbk.) — ISBN 978-1-4488-2635-3
  (6-pack)
  1. Nash, Steve, 1974—Juvenile literature. 2. Basketball players
  Canada—Biography—Juvenile literature. I. Title.
  GV884.N37O75 2011
  796.323092—dc22
  [B]
                            2010025265

Manufactured in the United States of America

CPSIA Compliance Information: Batch #WW11PK: For Further Information contact Rosen Publishing, New York, New York
at 1-800-237-9932

CONTENTS

Steve Nash is a basketball player.
He plays **point guard**.

Nash works well with his **teammates**. He is a team player.

Steve Nash was born on February 7, 1974, in Johannesburg, South Africa.

When he was a child, Nash moved to Canada. He is proud to be Canadian.

In 1996, Nash started playing for the Phoenix Suns.

In 1998, Nash was traded to the Dallas Mavericks. He became a star player in Dallas.

Nash returned to the Suns in 2004. He quickly became a team leader.

Nash was named the NBA's MVP, or most **valuable** player, in both 2005 and 2006.

19

Nash has many interests. He started a **foundation** that helps poor children.

Steve Nash loves basketball. He is a great player.

22

BOOKS

Here are more books to read about Steve Nash and basketball:

Areas, John. *Steve Nash*. NBA Readers. New York: Scholastic, 2008.

Medeiros, Michael de. *Steve Nash*. Remarkable People. New York: Weigl Publishers, 2008.

WEB SITES

Due to the changing nature of Internet links, PowerKids Press has developed an online list of Web sites related to the subject of this book. This site is updated regularly. Please use this link to access the list:
www.powerkidslinks.com/bmvp/stevena/

GLOSSARY

foundation (fown-DAY-shun) A group set up to give help a cause.

point guard (POYNT GAHRD) A basketball player who directs his or her team's forward plays on the court.

teammates (TEEM-mayts) People who play for the same team.

valuable (VAL-yoo-bul) Important.

INDEX